MW01240922

Weeping May Endure,

But Joy Comes in the Morning

by

Tenika Timpson

Text Copyright © 2021 by Tenika Timpson

All rights reserved. No part of this book may be reproduced, scanned, or distributed in any printed or electronic form or by any means without prior written consent of the publisher, except for brief quotes used in reviews.

Please do not participate in or encourage piracy of copyrighted materials in violation of the author's rights. Purchase only authorized editions.

Disclaimer: This book is a memoir. It reflects the author's present recollections of experiences over time. Some names and characteristics have been changed, some events have been compressed, and some dialogue has been recreated.

Published by

Hadassah's Crown Publishing, LLC

Library of Congress Control Number: 2021924131

ISBN 978-1-950894-63-5

Printed in the United States

I dedicate this book to my kids for enduring me through all of my trials and tribulations, even though my life is not perfect. I love you all with all of my well-being.

Contents

Introduction

1.	My Life	5
2.	My Passion	22
3.	Facing My Fears	23
4.	Going Back to What I Missed and More Disappointments in My Life	25
5.	Past Relationships and Experiences	28
6.	Family Betrayal	31
7.	Isolation	36
8.	Hating Doesn't Change a Thing	41
9.	Breaking the Silence	44
10.	Thinking the Impossible	47
11.	Overcoming Life-changing Secrets	49
12.	Breaking the Generational Curse	51
13.	Broken Spirits	53
14.	Being a Victim of Narcissism	56
15.	Sunshine After Darkness	60
16.	The Chosen Ones	67
17.	The Spiritual People Who Inspired Me	70
18.	Turning Back to Religion	73
19.	Learning How to Live in Peace	75

Acknowledgments	77
About the Author	79

Introduction

This book is inspired by God and dedicated to my four children and my boyfriend King, whom I love dearly. King has been my backbone since day one. He treats me like a queen, and he accepts me for me. Most of all, he loves and treats my children the same as he treats his children. I know I am blessed, but when God placed this man in my life, I then realized that it was nothing else that I needed, other than material things. God has many ways of answering prayers, giving rewards and showering us with blessings.

I hope this book will open the eyes of parents who don't pay attention to their children around people they tend to trust, especially family members and strangers. In this day and time, it is sad to say that people cannot be trusted. The very people you think you can trust and leave your kids with might be the very people who will take your child's innocence and childhood right under your nose.

If this has happened to you, or anyone in your family, know that you can overcome it by trusting in God? When you trust in God, you relieve that monster of the power they have over you. Just trust and keep faith in God, and He will handle the rest. So, parents, I know a break from your children sounds good, sometimes, but be very mindful of who is giving you that break because it can become a lifetime of horror for you and your children.

Chapter 1

My Life

Throughout my life, I always kept my children first, and this book was inspired by God to help me help others in my situation. And just know, I did everything in my power to prevent you all from any type of abusive situations, in your lives. I was born into a single-parent family as a child conceived by a married man. I always thought I knew who my father was until later in life. So just to make a long story short, I was born into a life of lies. But at the age of 21, the truth began to unfold when I learned of my real father. At the age of eight years old, I became a victim of sexual abuse by a close family member. I thought I was doing the right thing by telling Daisy, but that was the biggest mistake of my life. She did not say that she did not believe me, but her exact words were, "Stop. Don't say that!" and "Do not tell nobody else that!" Back in the old days, our ancestors did not want the law in their business. I knew then that I had to "look to the hills from which cometh my help."

Now, I had just admitted to Daisy what happened to me and did not receive any help. And there I was, a messed up, young and confused, lost child crying out for help. My childhood was gone in the blink of an eye. I was abused year after year after year, and it scared me to the point where I could not focus on being a child. I had nightmares for a long time. I gave up on trying to be a good child, so I started acting out and being disrespectful to Daisy because she hurt me. I thought that would be the only way to hurt her and get back at her because she was not there when I needed her.

I found myself hating Daisy and not caring about her, but I could not really hate her because, at the same time, she had problems of her own. She, in turn, was being abused and mistreated by her alcoholic husband. I had a little sister who was always treated like a princess, in my opinion. I always wondered why they treated her differently. I just accepted that I was nothing to Daisy because she let bad, filthy things happen to me, and she did not do anything but ignore me. Before all the bad things happened in my life, I was with a beautiful family that had me since I was a baby. That was the best part of my childhood, and that family taught me how to be nice and respectful. They took me in and treated me like I was a part of their family. At the age of 13, my life started getting a little easier because one of my cousins let me move in with her.

At the time, I thought it was a good thing, but after living with her for a while, I learned she had a problem, also. She was bipolar. She was nice some days, and then the next, she would be as mean as a bulldog. I didn't have a choice but to either leave or stay there, so I continued living there. I prayed a little harder and asked God to help me, and He answered my prayer. My cousin's attitude and problem improved, and I started helping her with her kids. She taught me how to keep my surroundings clean because she was a clean freak. At first, it freaked me out because she yelled if anyone left hair on the sink, but I got used to it. Overall, she was a blessing to me.

Throughout my childhood, God has placed me in the lives of some beautiful people. Life has its ways of throwing curve balls at times. For example, after being absent for some years, Daisy found her way back into my life. My cousin tried to tell me, "It's a trick. She doesn't love you. I took you in when she didn't want you." And I told her, "Yes you are so right, but she is still Daisy."

After I gave Daisy another chance and went back to her, it was okay for a while. I thought I'd forgiven her for what she allowed to happen to me. Evidently, I didn't forgive her because we started fighting and saying things to hurt each other's feelings, and one thing led to another. From that day on, our relationship began suffering and going downhill. I grew up and started hanging out. I tried to help another girl with her troubles and problems. She was not a stranger. I was told that she was my sister, so from that moment, I befriended her. She was mentally challenged and people always took advantage of her, using her to steal things from different stores for them. She did have a little sense, but sadly she used to perform sexual favors for a lot of men, mostly married men in my hometown, in this old hole-in-the-wall known as a "juke joint."

Time passed and we continued hanging out. We were in a terrible accident when she ran over one of the guys at a club who had ignored her. He almost lost his life that night because I saw him go up in the sky and come back down, leaving him with no skin on his body. I was so scared to get in the car with anybody for a long time because of the accident. For a while, that young man didn't talk to me because I was in the car that night. Years later, I saw him again. He was in a relationship with my best friend. She talked to him about me and we started talking again.

Life became a little brighter and better for me. I had a little bundle of joy, a baby girl and became engaged. Then it seemed like bad luck found me again when my best friend, some of her kids and her boyfriend were burned to death in a house fire. It seemed like a part of me died with her. Life threw me another curve ball when I ended up in a bad, abusive relationship with a man that she begged me to leave alone. I didn't listen because I thought that was love.

Turns out, I never knew what the word *love* meant. Soon, I ended up moving out of my apartment because I used to see my best friend in my apartment. My boyfriend Solomon moved me to some more apartments in a neighboring town. Again, that was not a good move. That man beat me so much that my body was immune to the beatings. I just gave up and thought that he beat me because he loved me. Afterall, that was all I saw when I was young. A friend told me that wasn't love. Solomon kept hitting me, although I was pregnant by him. He didn't care because I ended up losing our baby. I had a breakdown because I called Daisy and told her I needed her. She told me she couldn't be there for me. I left the hospital and wanted to end my life with pain pills. I called and told Solomon and he told me he was coming soon and to have his dinner ready. I told him I was under the doctor's care and on some heavy medicine, but he didn't care. I started cooking and fell asleep. The smoke almost took my life. But God had other plans for me, and he kept me a little longer.

Finally, I ended up leaving Solomon after all those years. I had a reality check and realized I had a beautiful baby girl waiting on me. Daisy did one good thing. She took care of my baby during the bad times in my life because I didn't want her to see what I was going through.

After that situation, I returned for my baby. With all that happened, I asked Daisy why she let that happen to me as a child. All she could say is, "How you know that it did not happen to me?" Then she dropped her head. From that instant, I knew I had to make peace with Daisy and let the past go. I knew that I would never forget what had happened to me as an innocent child. Years later, after I got over the man who hurt and scarred me, I released that sorrow because I was already a broken child looking for love in all the wrong places. In my earlier life, I had a lot of bad luck, bad relationships and deceptive people were all around me. Many women were a part of my journey, but God showed me that I had no friends because they used me and took advantage of me.

But God was always right there, and I was ignoring him and His signs. At times, I asked the Lord why bad things happened to me as a child, and why do people always take my friendship for granted? Life was alright for a while, and I started building another life for myself. I was blessed with two more children, and my life shifted. The man that I started life with treated me like a queen, at first, but he didn't realize what type of blessing God had sent in His life at that time. God challenged me and placed me in a position where I had to do what I was called to do. That was to take care of Julie, since she was my kids' grandmother. That was a true blessing from God because that woman taught me the true meaning of love and how to become a real woman. She taught me how to cook, how to carry myself as a woman, and she taught me my worth. I loved that lady like she was my mother, and her entire family took me in. I finally felt like I was where I was supposed to be. God showed me exactly why I was in that relationship. I wasn't sure if it was for my kids, but I wouldn't trade them for anything in this world. That woman became a best friend, and we did everything together. When you saw me, you saw her.

One day, God called His angel home. It was like a part of me died with Julie. It took me a while to get myself together. I then ran back to church begging God to help me. I did well for a while, but the devil got my attention again, and once again, I was lost. I started having sex with women, drinking, and partying just to avoid the hurt I was feeling inside. From there, I returned to the streets, jumped from job to job and got with the wrong crowd, trying to fit in. But that wasn't it. I started to think about all the good people I had wronged, but I didn't know how to apologize to them. So I did what I thought was right, and I isolated myself from everyone. I thought I had put everything behind me so I could move on to the next level in my life. Well, the next level wasn't a good level. The devil used me and introduced me to an older woman and tried to mold me into being like her. In the end, she became jealous of me. If only she had known that I looked at her as a genuine person, only to find out she was just like everybody else who used me and thought I was slow. Not only did she treat me like I was slow, she told people I was slow. That woman went behind me with my guy friends and still envied me.

The thing about too many people is they want what you have, and they will talk down about you because in reality, they want to be you. And that person doesn't know what you had to go through to get what you have, even though every blessing comes with a burden.

After a while, I thought I finally got the message God was telling me. "Life is what you make it." Time after time, I was winning in certain parts of my life. I had so many Christians wanting to be Christians and a lot more fake people to enter my life. Then, my life grew dark from being around the wrong people, but what I didn't know was that family can be your worst enemy. I had family members who I thought loved me, but they only kept me in their lives because I was the only person who dealt with them and their childish games. I lost a lot of people in my life because of the company I kept. I was nothing like them but being around them made me start acting like them, in some ways. I started doing things God wasn't proud of and I know he wouldn't have approved of. But one thing I learned. You have to have faith and keep God as your number one priority. I found out that God never left my side, and no matter whether it was good or bad, He always brought me through the hard trials.

After a while, I thought I cheated death because I was in so many situations when I could have lost my life. I found myself with a man who cheated on me and disrespected me when he was drinking alcohol. One day, I prayed and asked God to show me if this man was for me, and God did just that one thing. The devil got inside of him one day, and he put his hands on me. I promised myself I would not let another man hit me. He slapped me and I told him I didn't want him anymore. At that instant, he drew a gun to my face and was about to pull the trigger. From that moment, I realized and I said to myself, "God, if you let me make it through this, I'm leaving him." And, I did.

Afterwards, I was single for a while. My God is an awesome God. Years later, I met Billy, the love of my life, and I didn't have much time with him, but the little time I did spend with him was remarkable and left me speechless. We had our bad days and good days, but one thing I can say, the good days outweighed the bad. Again, God had more plans for me and I was blessed with another beautiful, baby girl who is the spitting image of Billy. We weren't together, but we were talking about getting back together, then God called His angel home. That was a hard pill to swallow because on the day Billy passed, he and I had an argument and we both said some ugly things to each other.

There's not one day that goes by that I don't regret our last conversation. I never had a chance to tell Billy I was sorry and didn't mean any of the things I said to him. God has mysterious ways of opening our eyes. Months before my baby's father passed, I was hospitalized for pancreatitis. I learned then while I was in the hospital alone that I had to get my life together because God had given me too many chances. God pulled me through that scary time in my life, and I realized I only have a few people who care about me. I'm grateful for the people who helped me during that time in my life.

Fortunately, God healed me, and I got well after my breakup from a married man. He was separated from his wife, and the man was good to my kids and me. There wasn't anything I wanted that he wouldn't give me. But with that being said, God had to show me signs that he wasn't the one for me.

God has his own timing for everything because after being single for eight months, He gave me my own man. This guy and I clicked, at first sight. I didn't believe in love at first sight, but at that moment, my life changed in the blink of an eye. This man became my best friend and he had my back no matter how the devil tried to separate us. King and I became so attached to one another that we started finishing each other's sentences and thoughts. I knew he was a blessing from God because my life is a fairy tale with him. Believe it or not, we never argue or fight, but I'm not saying we don't disagree on certain things. In the end, he's usually right.

God again answered my prayers. Everything I prayed for in my next relationship, God blessed me with it. I was always told that behind every blessing is a burden because even though I had the perfect man for me, I gained haters. There were people disliking me because I left all my so-called friends alone. My life was getting stressful by the day because my friends always said, "You are with your boyfriend all the time. You act funny. You think you are better than us." That wasn't the problem at all. I was tired of being around jealousy, negativity and people who envied me because I didn't have anything they didn't have.

I might have taken care of what I had, but I never was the jealous type. I always tried to fit in because I wanted to feel like somebody. What these people didn't know is that I had a terrible childhood and they seemed to always be happy. Their parents loved them unconditionally, gave them the world and taught them and raised them better than they showed and acted. I distanced myself from many people that I would do anything for and had their backs since we were school kids because I thought they would be happy for me. Instead, they were fatally attracted to me. Additionally, someone told them I was gossiping about them. Sometimes, we have to separate ourselves from people when we find out they're not really for us. To tell the truth about the situation, I moved on with my life, distanced myself and made a lot of personal sacrifices in order to work on myself.

Talk about stepping out on faith. Yes, I did. Out of the blue, I started receiving harassing phone calls. It was like some Lifetime Movie Network story. I found my car scratched up and egged, which was very childish. I was upset and hurt because I worked hard for my possessions. It got worse when King started receiving harassing phone calls. The caller would say nasty, filthy things about me which were not true. But guess what? He did not fall for it because he never got a phone call before when we were cool, so he didn't fall for those childish games. That's the difference between a grown man and a boy. I had to make reports to the authorities.

At that point, I was fed up and tired because I didn't bother anybody. The thing about gossiping is that you cannot stop people from talking about you. I started praying even harder, but stuff continued to happen. It reached the point where the person persuaded an innocent person to get involved. I really couldn't say anything because I was a people pleaser. I never could say "no" and didn't care what it was. Not once did I think about the impact it would have on the innocent person. I thank God for opening my eyes and enabling me to identify my discernment as a part of my healing process. As I got older, I learned to enjoy my quality of life by putting God first in all I did. And when you have God in every space and crack in your life, your misery evaporates and you become carefree.

If I hadn't read the novel *Miracle In My Mouth* by Rainie Howard I would still be confused about the things that are going on in my life. I also have two other people I converse with who have taught me about life and the vibrations and the energies within our lives. In the end, I learned my lesson to always guard my heart from negativity and pray and ask God to forgive me for the bitterness, hatred and jealousy in my heart and keep the faith because God loves me no matter what I have done or do, and He will never leave me nor forsake me.

Chapter 2

My Passion

My passion is caring for and assisting others. It makes me feel good to give back to others as God has given to me. So if I can help somebody by taking them to the store or picking up their medicines from the grocery store, I will. I know that it is hard to depend on people to help you on a long-term basis. If you don't believe me, get sick and find out. I know by blessing others, God will continue to bless me. He has proven this to me over and over in my life. I don't boast or brag or care to be noticed for what I do for others. Just know that what I do is from the goodness of my heart. Don't get me wrong. People will try to use you. But when I see it coming, I clear my path fast, and then I eliminate myself before it becomes a problem or too much to handle.

Chapter 3

Facing My Fears

The first molestation incident happened when I was left alone with a family member at Daisy's house. He approached me when I was in bed asleep and said, "I will kill you if you tell anybody what happens when we are together." Then he preceded to force himself inside my anal cavity as I laid on my stomach. I cried and screamed for Daisy and she wasn't there to protect me. When he was done doing the devil's work, he just threw the cover over me; I didn't feel like the little princess I was anymore.

At eight years old, many thoughts ran through my mind, like why is this my blood relative. But I knew I could not overpower a full-grown man I was just helpless and this was only the beginning. I remember another time it happened at Penny's house in her living room. I was bent over to the point where I was being invaded, and I bit into her couch to take away some of the pain and pressure from my body. I cried, even though I knew it wasn't doing any good.

I went to Penny because I just knew that I could be safe at her house. But she had to work that particular morning and I loved going to spend time with my cousin. She didn't like me being around because she was the only little girl Penny had at the time. I thought she would let me get in bed with her, but she didn't. That's how I ended up on the living room chair. Shortly after that, I expressed to Penny what happened to me, but guess what? That didn't help because then I thought, well now, I know my favorite aunt, whom I loved so much, didn't care about me either. I felt alone and just did anything for attention.

I felt nobody cared because they were so wrapped up in their own lives. Daisy didn't pay attention to her child and what was going on in her household. Because my home was not safe any longer, I was lost in my mind and soul. I was literally a bomb waiting to explode, with all sorts of feelings bottled up inside.

Chapter 4

Going Back to What I Missed and More Disappointments....

I returned to school and received my high school diploma. I attended Strayer University to study business administration for two years. I also attended Piedmont Technical College for three years. I didn't finish because I was diagnosed with vertigo, which is being consumed by feeling fatigued, having motion sickness and anxiety, all because of what happened to me as a child.

Every girl dreams of the perfect, fairytale life. They dream of being educated and saving their virginity for the perfect man. They dream of marrying the man who will take care of them. They both will be successful and live in a large home with a white, picket fence. They dream of having a perfect family and that their kids will be successful, as well. But we all know 'that' life only comes around for one in a million people. So just like every other girl who dreams, I did the same, but as you can see, my life turned out nothing of the sort. Just because our lives don't turn out the way we planned, it doesn't make us bad people.

Life is full of experiences, disappointments, struggles and lessons to be learned as we travel down life's highways. So even though we become disappointed with ourselves for whatever we don't achieve, we will come to realize that we have seasons in life. There is a season for everything and everything happens for a reason. So, if you don't become a millionaire, maybe it was predestined that God knew you weren't able to handle it. Some people are born into fortune, but these are the few lucky ones. The good and the bad trials and tribulations of your life should be lessons learned, as they evaporate. So, this is where we are able to tell our kids, grandkids and great grandkids the right way to live. We can't tell them anything if we have never been through anything. That's just like the perfect preacher getting up to preach. If you are perfect, what can you tell me? So don't dwell on the negative.

Always find the positive that comes out of a negative situation. Always hold yourself accountable and responsible for your actions. Because just when you think life has dealt you an ugly hand, just look around at the world today. I guarantee there's somebody else out there who has it a lot worse than you do. There are all kinds of struggles in life, whether they are financial, relationship, sexuality, mental, physical, psychological, or emotional. And if you are not a perfect person, you fall into one of these categories. The only way you don't is if you just don't admit it. We all know there is only one perfect man, and we are far from that.

Chapter 5

Past Relationships and Experiences

This journey was a lifetime experience that I will never forget. I became involved with a guy who taught me a lot about life and how to feel like a celebrity. At least that is what all the girls in a neighboring county thought. All the girls were in love with him, but guess what? I got in a relationship with him and had two kids by him. Have you ever watched a movie and a scene appeared that kept you on the edge of your seat? Well that's when my life was headed in the wrong direction, down the wrong lane. It's like I attracted guys who used women as punching bags, and they trained them and made them the way they wanted them to be.

Now, I did have some good days, but again the bad days outweighed the good days. Our relationship didn't work because we lost trust. We were fighting more than being happy and enjoying our kids and our lives. But one thing about that relationship that was a life changing step for me was his mom becoming my best friend. My kids' grandmother Julie taught me everything I know from cooking, taking care of my kids and becoming the woman I am today. She became sick. I took care of her when I was able to, but she eventually passed away and a part of me left with her. I was lost for a while because I didn't have anybody to confide in and share my dark secrets and daily problems with.

My relationship with her son lasted for about nine and-a-half years, on and off, because of the violence, abuse and lies. We finally decided to go our separate ways, but for some reason we had a bond no one could tear apart.

Grown people do grown things. I cannot live my life by the judgement of humans. There are people who keep fantasies in their minds and there are people who act on them. I am one who will act on them because I am grown. Role playing, dressing up, and flogging are some things that are frowned upon, by most. But don't knock it until you try it. A vast few of us get bored by doing the same stuff all the time on a different day. So yes, I'm different, but I'm honest and I learned to love a spiced-up life. That guy took me to a whole entire level where I felt I was in control, and for some reason, I liked it. It turned me on. He was a charmer, but he didn't play any games. He loved women, but I thought he loved me more. I knew that I was lost in the world. It was fun at first, but it got old and then our bond started breaking. After that episode, I thought I was like a pro at reaching the next level in relationships. I started giving advice to other women. Finally, I knew that I had to think on another level in my entire life, and I did.

Chapter 6

Family Betrayal

Life just wasn't easy for me. I had a younger cousin who I love so much. There wasn't anything we didn't do together. We went on double dates, vacations; you name it, we did it. We had each other's backs and we showed each other that we loved one another. Everyone said we looked like twins, which we did, especially when our hair was styled the same way. She was like a sister, more than a cousin to me. Even when we started having kids, we still kept in touch with one another. I was close with a lot of my cousins on my dad's side, also.

I had another cousin who I befriended on my dad's side who I hung out with like a sister. She taught me a valuable lesson about choosing who I hung out with. I don't know if she was obsessed with jealousy or what. This chick did stuff that only occurred on the Lifetime Channel, at least I thought. She looked out for me, a lot, but I also did the same for her if I could. But for some reason she turned on me because of the lies people told her I said about her.

Sometimes, the things people told her that I said weren't lies, but there's nobody that could tell her that I told things we did in our younger days. Now, the older we became, the more distant we became because of some of the things she was doing. Some were illegal and some were just low down and dirty.

As soon as I started using the brain God gave me, I finally stopped dealing with her because I found out she was the one talking about me behind my back. She lied and said I was doing witchcraft and evil things to people. I was introduced to it, but I didn't have faith in it. I closed that door and asked God to forgive me for even bringing that type of ungodly stuff in my life. It even got so bad that I finally gossiped about my cousin, and it got back to her. But one person can't talk by themselves. If so, there is something wrong with them. My cousin was so mad at me that she called around trying to turn people against me. She persuaded one of her friends to help her egg and scratch up my car. I'm telling you that life is not fair and has never really been to me. I tried reaching out to her family and she had told them I was lying. I even went to the police and nothing happened. I don't know what kind of spiritual witchcraft she knew, but I took that loss and went on with my life.

God has kept me safe and protected my kids and me, and all I'm saying is don't ignore the signs that God puts in your face about people. Never worry about the dead people. They can't hurt you. It's the ones you keep close to you. This chick was the type that felt if she disliked a certain individual that I had to dislike the same individual just because I hung out with her. This is just an example of the power that she wanted to have over me.

Family is all the descendants of a common ancestor, but you can meet people that will treat you better than family. If you give your life to God, He will place people in your path that you never thought you would be dealing with. Believe it or not, sometimes others and strangers treat you better than family. Don't get me wrong. I do love my family, but once I form a special bond with you and realize that you are not loyal, I close the chapter on that book. I will forgive, but I won't forget.

When I met my final baby's father, he was young, vibrant, and I was in love. I met him on this job that we worked at together. I thought I had it right this time, but this relationship was short lived. I became pregnant with my last daughter, Princess, only to find out that he did not want kids. Well, it was too late for that. I finally realized this guy wasn't ready for what I was ready for, so we parted ways and he passed away after the first two years of Princess' life. That was a sad time in my life because even though he didn't want any kids at first, Princess turned out being his "lil mama." And she is his twin. They look just alike.

Before he passed away, he had three beautiful little girls, and my baby girl was the oldest. My baby's father and I didn't always see eye to eye, but when it came down to my child, neither one of us played any games. Most of all, with him being gone, my baby is trying to keep in touch with her sisters, being that she is the oldest. He was a great father, even though he was young. He said I made him a man, meaning I made him become a man. Little did he know he was already a mature young man who didn't act his age, and he was very respectful and very protective of his kids and family. Older people say that when someone looks like their mother and father and they die, the words they say are, "he's not gone; he left those beautiful three little girls behind." And when you look at my baby you see nothing but him. When he first passed, my baby was alright because she didn't know what was going on and what happened.

When she turned three, she started missing him more and the days got harder. At the age of four, she finally started realizing that her dad was gone to heaven, but she used to always ask is daddy coming back? All I could do was look in her glossy beautiful little eyes and say, "Baby, you will see daddy again one day. That was a difficult time in my life."

Chapter 7

Isolation

I can finally live a life free of drama and unhappiness. When my life was full of drama, it was because of some of the company I kept around. I was the girl in school who always fit in and had friends, but I was so confused and lost in school that I began to want to be alone. School was one of my ways to escape from home because of the abuse that I had to deal with from my stepfather who was always fighting and fussing with Daisy because of the alcoholic beverages he chugged down daily. I had a little sister who I loved so much. She was like a fat-cheeked, black baby doll. But I grew to envy her because as she got older, she became a little spoiled brat who was never fussed at. She never did anything wrong, so I got used to it. It began to grow on me that it wasn't her fault; she was an innocent child.

One time my little sister turned a pot of hot beans on

herself, and it burned parts of her body. Thankfully, she was okay and the burns were not life-threatening. She was her parents' little princess that they catered to and made sure she was great with everything. I didn't treat her badly after that happened. I held her, rocked her and cried, not because she was hurt, but because of how Daisy was there for her. I felt she was never there for me in the same way.

Because of my relationship with Daisy, I did everything I could to stay away from home. In school, I tried running track, but I couldn't run that much due to my irregular heartbeat. Next, I tried out for basketball, not knowing anything about the sport. I was just trying to occupy my time and trying to stay away from home as much as possible.

After a while, I connected with a girl who showed me how to really have fun, or so I thought. She taught me how to skip school, party and then get back to school before the bus arrived. This got old, and I eventually stopped and started hanging with a friendly girl that was faster than me. I stepped out of my comfort zone and started going mud riding, drag racing, and to see chicken fights. I actually enjoyed being with her family. They treated me like I was one of them.

Like too many of my classmates, I didn't graduate from high school. I had to drop out of school because of my illness. I broke out in whelps when I left home because I was afraid of what would happen to Daisy while I was gone. Not only did her boyfriend beat her, he beat me as well. My oldest cousin defended me after I told him about it. And he never touched me again after that day. My cousin was my hero, but he had his own life and wasn't around much. Penny defended Daisy on different occasions, but Daisy loved that man so much. The police removed us from the home, but Daisy took us back. I didn't understand what was going on.

By the time I was 13, my family and I had been through three homes for abused families. You know what they say; you shouldn't judge a book by its cover. Well, I have always been judged since the day I entered this world. The devil has always tried to take me, but I thank God that I am one of the chosen ones. I was always sweet and humble, but I did some things in my life that I am not proud of. But tell me one person who has never made a mistake and done something that they regretted once they understood that it was wrong. It took me a long time to learn what was wrong and what was right because I was always doing something wrong. I knew it was bad, but I was a people pleaser. Whatever somebody asked, I was always willing to do. I didn't know how to say "no" until it was too late.

By age 14, I took it upon myself to move out of my parents' house and to go live with one of my oldest cousins. Life got a little better for me. I was at peace for a moment, until life started setting in on me and I knew that I couldn't live with her for the rest of my life. I got a job so I could start saving money, but instead the money was coming in fast, and all we did was shop, play cards and throw parties. That was fun for a minute, but then I still felt empty inside. I felt empty inside because I didn't look like what I had been through. People always looked at me like I had it all and had the best life, all because I wore nice clothes and had my hair done nicely.

But little did they know, I was always running a race in my own life. I actually felt I was competing against myself. That's why I never was jealous of wanting to be like someone else when I was young. I didn't have a childhood except for a short period of time because sexual abuse makes you grow up fast. These episodes lasted until I was 14 years of age. I guess I prayed and cried every night as I got on my knees asking God to save me because I couldn't take anymore. I couldn't let one more person do me wrong because, at that time, if another bad thing happened to me, I probably would have taken my own life. As I grew older, I started feeling bad about the things that I had done to hurt people, even many years ago.

Chapter 8

Hating Doesn't Change Anything

Hating someone does not hurt them. I noticed that it was only hurting me. God tells us to forgive people just as he has forgiven us. It took me a long time walking in a straight line. I started doing everything the way God wanted me to so I could become who He designed me to be. For example, the people that used to hurt me, I used to fight in order to hurt them. I learned that fighting did not solve anything. The older I got, the fighting became worse, and I realized this was only going to land me in jail or prison. Because of my kids, I stopped.

I struggled for a while because all kinds of obstacles came my way. Temptation continued knocking on my door. I was so confused and frustrated that I started going to different churches because I thought maybe I wasn't getting the message right. But that wasn't it. I experienced so many new things about the Bible and other religions. I remember when God was working on me to the point I was walking the line so straight as a Christian, I stopped having sex, drinking, thinking negative and using bad language. Now, let me tell you that it was so hard for me. I did it so long that I experienced the next level of being a Christian, as a believer. I experienced the holy ghost and began speaking in tongues, and I thought my life had changed for good. That wasn't the case at all. I ended up missing the world, so I went back to my old life. But I still felt that I wasn't going to let God down, so I didn't drink, party, say or think any negative things, for a while. That part was hard for me because I was used to the worldly things.

Being a Christian is not easy and there's nothing you can do overnight. It can be very stressful and frustrating. But I finally learned that God forgives and He loves me no matter what. And the devil is always around, so the best thing for me is to stay prayed up, stay in The Word and stay positive. God will protect me and keep me in my peace. God is the person that can make things happen in your life, not anything or

anyone else other than yourself, with the grace and the

blessings of God.

Chapter 9

Breaking the Silence

When dealing with a problem such as mine, a lot of family members say, "What happens in this family stays in this family." Enough of that stuff. That's why the world is messed up today. Silence is what makes criminals and psychopaths bottle their problems up; it only causes stress, and stress can kill you. We are no longer in the age where everything has to be hidden. I know you have seen the *Me Too Act* come out recently. This is where people are coming out about their personal experiences with sexual abuse. It may have been buried for years since it happened, but now people are coming forth and talking about it. Believe it or not, priests and boy scout leaders have been at the top of the list as sexual predators.

I learned from being molested at an early age that most people will not confront their problems because of their pride and shame. They would rather take it to their grave than to have their problems resurface. These secrets will become skeletons in their closets and sometimes weigh very heavily on their minds. People don't realize they will face problems such as depression, anxiety, PTSD, and other related illnesses. One can be affected mentally, physically, emotionally, and psychologically. One may have nightmares, night sweats, eating disorders and other related symptoms of stress. So it is really imperative to find a positive coping mechanism to help get you through your problems.

Some people meditate, some people go through therapy, and some people choose a higher power to help them. For me, I chose a higher power, which is God. I pray and meditate daily, and I'm also prescribed medication to help me focus. This is nothing to be ashamed of. I am working on myself. When you think of hiding, covering up things, as you continue to build, the mountain becomes larger and larger. What do you think will happen next? Yes, you will come tumbling down. So when you start hiding your problems and things that have happened to you in life, it is not healthy.

First you have to identify that you have a problem before it

can ever be solved. This reminds me of the Serenity Prayer.

The Serenity prayer simply says, "God grant me the serenity

to accept the things that I cannot change, to change the

things that I can, and the wisdom to know the difference."

Chapter 10

Thinking the Impossible

Who would have thought their mother envied them. Nobody! Exactly. But I think Daisy envies me because of her actions I observed growing up as her daughter. Daisy envying me has been a negative and unfortunate situation over the course of my life. I would rather have a person in the street envy me than Daisy. I say Daisy feels some type of way because we began to clash a lot of times when I felt that Daisy just wasn't there for me as I expected her to be, especially after I told her about the sexual abuse. I didn't intentionally try to disrespect her, but I had a lot of resentment inside of me.

My mother was all I had. I expected her to approach the situation differently, and I felt a sense of shock because it seemed as though my backbone just didn't have me. Then I felt a form of hate, rage and self-worthlessness. To sum it up, it seems as though she didn't care if she didn't show me that she cared. At this point, I felt I was alone on an island surrounded by nothing but water with no help. I did what any other child that didn't know what to do would do. I lashed out and just didn't have any respect left for Daisy. At this point, I just thought this wouldn't be happening to me. I felt I was on the outside looking in. This is the type of stuff I experienced in my lifetime.

Chapter 11

Overcoming Life-changing Secrets

During life, some kids grow up with two parents in a good home with structure and become productive adults. In some cases, kids are reared in a single-parent home in the same manner and become productive adults. There are other cases where the home is dysfunctional and kids have no structure; therefore, their quality of life is damaged from their upbringing. My story comes from being a child raised in a dysfunctional home. From birth until the age of eight I had a normal childhood.

At the age of eight, my life took a turn. I began to be sexually abused by a family member. It all started when Daisy started leaving me with a family member and neglecting me to go gambling. She left me with someone that she trusted. As a young and innocent little girl, I did not know what was going on. The pain was excruciating and I know it was unbearable for a grown woman to bear.

Some moms do not pay attention to their households. It is a shame when a mother puts an addiction before her child. It had gotten so bad she would gamble daily, not knowing what doors the devil had opened up right under her nose. It is scary to be young and have your life threatened by a family member if you tell someone what happened while your caretaker is gone. Daisy was so in the streets with what they called, back in the day, "poker machines" that she invited the devil to live under the same roof as me.

Right then and there my childhood was robbed and my life became hell, while Daisy was happy winning or losing her money. And little did she know, she was also losing her child, too. From that day, I began disliking and being around Daisy. To feel safe, I started asking to go to friends' and other family members' houses.

Chapter 12

Breaking the Generational Curses

Life's experiences taught me how to be security-minded. This means, I am always aware of my surroundings and my kids' surroundings. I am not quick to trust anybody. I have to build a solid rapport with anyone that I let into my small circle. If you cross me one time, it is over. I watch the people that my kids deal with and study them, and if I feel like danger is near, I won't let them engage with others.

Sometimes, I feel it is unfair, but I'd rather be safe than sorry. And I am also instilling in them to not trust their kids around everybody because they know my situation. So when they ask questions, I am open and honest with them; I don't try to hide information about pedophilia. There is no rule in my house that states, "Whatever goes on in this house, stays in this house." Parents need to stop telling their kids this. If something is wrong, they should want it to be exposed.

Parents should take the time to talk to their kids and educate them about pedophilia, assuring them that if they tell, they will be protected. If this is practiced, I believe there will be fewer cases of sexual abuse in the future.

Chapter 13

Broken Spirits

Broken spirits mean you have lost hope, courage and the will to fight for yourself or anyone. Having a broken spirit can come from constantly being abused physically, mentally, verbally, emotionally and spiritually. To have your mind, heart, faith and body broken is painful and devastating to a young, innocent child who can't defend himself or herself. I guess you're wondering how I could go through all of that at an early age and carry that pain and misery around with me all those years.

Well, I overcame all the pain, misery, and shame. As I grew older, I realized that my illnesses came from the stress and all the pain that I carried with me for so long. What I want to tell children and teenagers going through this same pain is don't give up and continue praying and asking God to remove the pain from your life in a pleasant way. And just because you are going through this, don't run from God; run to Him because everything happens for a reason. We all go through trials and tribulations to make us strong, so we can help someone else.

What I had to realize is that after all these years, my past childhood of molestation and misery were still there. I didn't forgive Daisy and family members for all that I went through when I was young. For future reference, pay attention to the signs that people give you, and parents, don't be so quick to trust anyone with your children these days.

 Satan is a spirit that you will not recognize. I didn't know what the word "narcissist" was when I was young, but I was a victim of narcissism. I was taken advantage of as a child by an adult family member. To me, Satan and narcissists can be very manipulative and can easily control your mind when you are at the age when you don't understand what's going on in your life. Trust no one but God; He will be there, even when bad things are happening in your life.

God never said we wouldn't have to go through anything,

but He did say He will never leave us nor forsake us. I'm a living witness because throughout my life, when I was old enough to know right from wrong, I still chose to do wrong. And also, guess what? God was there to pull me out every time I needed him. When I was sick, he made sure my kids and I were never hungry or without lights and shelter.

So, the way I look at life now is that life is what you make it. Yes, once someone's spirit has been crushed or damaged it can be restored. With God on your side, all things are possible. Give it all to God and see what happens in your life next. I did and look at me now; my dream of becoming a business owner has come true. God gave me the strength to tell my testimony by writing this book about my childhood. And I was able to overcome because I trusted and had God by my side.

Chapter 14

Being A Victim of Narcissism

Narcissism, to me, is dysfunctional. I have been a victim of narcissism my entire life. When I was young and after the molestation, abuse and being in an abusive family, I began having tantrums and fits of rage. When I reached the age of understanding, I knew I was having narcissistic rage, which is a reaction to narcissistic injury. Being a victim of narcissism can make you have depressive episodes, paranoid delusions, outbursts and violent attacks. I remember when I started having violent outbursts and unstoppable rages. Daisy tried to have me committed to a mental institution in Augusta, Georgia. But I will tell you that God is good. Even though I wanted to be committed to that place, after I took a test and passed it, they said there wasn't anything wrong with me. At that point, I started thinking Daisy didn't want me around anymore because of my behavior. But little did she know, my emotional behavior was because she never paid me any attention and was not there for me when I needed her the most after I was being molested.

Narcissists have two layers of rage. The first layer of rage can be when a person has constant anger towards someone else, and the second layer is having self-aimed anger. Not only was I a victim of narcissism, I was raised by a narcissistic parent. I recall asking Daisy, after I got older, why she didn't protect me and do anything about my molester after I confided in her? Her words were, "How do you know it didn't happen to me?" At that moment, I knew that Daisy had gone through something in her life that she was ashamed to admit. Now that I'm older, Daisy thinks she needs to know my every move and to be close to me. I believe Daisy feels threatened by my independence. This is a pattern of narcissistic attachment, when the parent considers that the child exists solely to fulfill their needs and wishes. Mom often tries to control my life. She always crossed my boundaries by trying to be in my personal business, being messy, and speaking negatively about me at all times. I have been manipulated by Daisy my entire life. That is, until I started loving her from a distance.

Now let me explain something. I love Daisy and she loves me, but these are my feelings, and this is how I have to close the molestation chapter of my life. Also, writing this book wasn't easy for me. I'm not bashing Daisy; I'm just expressing my feelings and healing from all the hurt and pain that I endured in my past. I cannot carry this burden around any longer. The molestation had a big impact on my life; it silenced me for years, and then it started affecting me inside and out. I was always stressed and had low self-esteem, but I asked God to help me by directing my path.

As I grew older, I no longer blamed Daisy and the family member because he was dead. But I brought destruction upon my own life once I became of age by making bad and wrong decisions. All I'm saying is narcissism is real, and it can ruin anyone's life. It destroy relationships between mothers and daughters, fathers and sons, etc. I don't blame Daisy anymore. I had to sit back and realize that Daisy was also human, and that she was victimized and never received any help. That's why she had problems and family issues.

I really hope that readers of my book are empowered to overcome whatever issues they have been through. Know that you are not alone, and there are more women and men who have been victimized. Also, I hope my example teaches and helps someone who has been through molestation to identify when darkness approaches their lives.

Life never gave me a chance. That's what I thought until one day, Ms. Bridget Martin came across my path through Facebook. At that moment, I tell you God is good. The message she was speaking on is what I needed to hear. I connected with her because she has been through some of the things that, not only I, but millions of others all over the world have been through. Her message set me free and helped me a great bit.

Chapter 15

The Sunshine After Darkness

I dangled for a while and had little flings, as I longed for a good man. Someone told me to pray for a good man and be specific, if that's what I really wanted. They also said, "But you have to leave these little boys alone." And I asked her, "What do you mean?" My friend said that I needed to also be ready because a real grown man will look past the fact that I have four children. He will still take care of and love your kids. I got myself together and started focusing on my family.

One day, I was at the gas station and saw this man that I knew from my childhood, but he was a grown man now. King was tall, dark and handsome and we walked past each other. We didn't notice each other until he came back out of the store. Then, we approached each other and reconnected. We embraced each other in a hug and he said, "I'll see you soon." My fast, flirty self said, "We will see each other sooner than you think!" King smelled so good I hated to let him go. I just had to see him again, so his brother invited me to a cookout the following weekend. I couldn't wait to see this man again, so the following week I arranged to get my hair and nails done, and to get the perfect outfit, in order to be ready for this cookout.

I attended the cookout on that Saturday afternoon as scheduled, and oh my God, there he was. I took one look and said I'm going to make this my man. We started talking, mingling and dancing at the cookout. After about two drinks, I knew I had to hold my composure. I said to myself, "Easy girl, easy!" We stepped outside for some air and started talking and before I knew it, his lips were against mine. I had to stop kissing him and jump back before I lost my composure. I knew I had to get away. After quickly exchanging numbers, I left. We talked on the telephone over the next couple of weeks and finally, we set up a date. We both understood that we were going to be friends having fun with no strings attached. We learned that we had so much in common, but we were two totally different people.

One day, we finally connected, and oh my God, King blew my mind! My friend still picks on me today about my next day's reaction. I had to tell somebody that my life and my body have never been the same. Our conversations and our relationship have been phenomenal. I want to go into depth because it is indescribable. We started our relationship with no strings attached, for fun, but only God controls love. I am in a committed relationship with this man. I love him and he loves me. He accepted my kids and they respect him. I also love his kids and treat them like they are mine, even though I only met one of them. His son connected with me the first time I met him, and that meant a lot to him and me. His son is so respectful, and I enjoy every moment we spend together. Princess' father passed away, so after I was with him for a while, she asked him, "Will you be my dad because I don't have one?" His reaction was unbelievable. He told her, "Baby, you have a dad. He's just not here anymore, but I will step in that place and be your father." And from that day forward, she has had another father. God showed up and showed out when he placed this man in our lives. We never have had an argument or a fight; it's just like a fairytale.

This man is my best friend. I can talk to him about anything, and we can do anything together. This man has had my back, since day one. He makes sure I have what I need, and he keeps me on track with finances, daily life struggles and problems. I can say, all our good days outweigh the bad days because there never have been any bad days. This man never judges me nor turns his back on me. My kids are grateful for that. We connect physically, but I'm not clingy to this man. We give each other time from one another or "me time." This is our time to breathe and to think or go out with the guys or the girls. Some times, he goes fishing alone because it's so peaceful. At other times, I also go fishing with him. There is nothing we haven't done together that I can think of. We go out together just to get away for a while.

Until I met this man, I was not living; I was only existing. We go on family vacations, personal vacations, date nights, and we cook for each other and the family. He takes care of me when I'm sick, and when he's sick, I take care of him. We give each other gifts just because and we also go to church together. I didn't know it then, but I know now this is the man that I prayed to God for, and I was specific. I can't say what the future holds, but I have a promise ring. And if it gets any better than this, I don't know what I'm going to do with myself.

Now my kids feel like I have failed them as a mother, but little do they know, everything I have done and endured is for them. I live for my kids to make sure their lives are better than mine. I know my kids' anger, anxiety and stress come from the household I had them growing up in when they were younger. If Daisy had left me with the family that raised me from a baby and never came back, my kids' lives would have been better because they would never have been in homes where they had to see me fight and get thrown out of our home. I was raised by three sisters, and sometimes their mom helped with me, also. I was better off there. I was loved and never had to worry about anything bad happening to me. They taught me to be respectful, to love and just be a kid. I was around kids all the time. I was there so long, I started calling them "Ma" and "Big Ma." I loved them so much. Those ladies took care of me like I was their child. There was nothing that I didn't have. Food wasn't a problem. We ate from the garden and the men in the family killed the meat; we ate well. All their kids were like my brothers and sisters, and they loved me like I was their sister, as well.

But one thing I can say is they never looked over me; they showed me love and took good care of me. I used to wonder where Daisy was, but after I didn't see her for a while, I just forgot about her and started calling her by her middle name. It was never by her correct title again. That family will always have a special place in my heart and especially their kids because they took me places with them and showed me love. I love my kids, and there's nothing I wouldn't do for them. One thing they can't ever say is that I never let anything happen to them, and I don't ever plan on letting anything happen to them while I'm living and can protect them. I don't blame anyone anymore for what happened to me, and I love all my family and Daisy. I forgive those who I reached out to for help and the ones who didn't care. I gave it all to God, and I finally realized that this was not my battle to fight any longer. Every day in my prayers, I thank God for the experience that I endured in life.

I'm not proud of all of them, but I do not regret them. This was my stairway to becoming the woman that I am today. I might not be what I should be, but I thank God I'm not what I used to be. Through all my trials and tribulations, I had to learn to put God first, and when you pray and be specific, God will deliver. He brought me from the streets, from bad relationships and let me overcome obstacles in my life. He gave me the ability to forgive. Now I can live my life to the fullest and not allow my past to predict my future.

Chapter 16

The Chosen Ones

The reason I call myself "one of the chosen ones" is because I have a calling on my life. If something has never happened to you, how can you teach and tell somebody else about that in order to stop them from experiencing that same thing ? I was always told that I had an anointing on my life. I remember when I used to dream things before they happened. I would be scared to death.

There was a time in my life when I saw dead people. I thought I was hallucinating, so I started getting advice from different people, which was the wrong thing to do. I should have just prayed and asked God to show me what was going on. I learned that I wasn't one of the chosen ones. I'm just a young lady who endured things that some other young woman went through in their lives, also. I also had to learn that everyone has trials and tribulations in their lives. Some people will open up and some people will not. Since I think my testimony will help someone else, I decided to open up. Because of what happened to me, I have trust and insecurity issues today. I keep a close, watchful eye on my kids, my friends, and my mate, period. All this is stemming from what happened to me as a child. I'm trying to show my readers the impact that abuse has had on my life. I don't understand people who say they don't believe in God because there has to be a God to deliver these people from these types of issues.

When you feel like you're at the end of life's rope, God will pick you up and make you stronger. Some people have relied on different coping mechanisms, such as drugs, alcohol, sex, and they may contemplate suicide. When you have God as your higher power, he will help you work through all of your troubles. I know this because I am a living witness. It makes me think about the song *Don't Judge My Praise If You Don't Know My Story*. That's why I'm glad we serve a merciful God. People will not let you forget your past, but once you ask God for forgiveness, it is over. If people

were the ones to judge, most would already be in hell.

Chapter 17

Spiritual People Who Inspired Me

The special person in my life I look up to is Joyce Meyer from Joyce Meyer's Ministries. That woman is powerful and strong. I wonder if she knows how she has changed so many people's lives? I know she definitely changed mine. I remember Joyce Meyer spoke about her father molesting her, but she didn't hate him for it; she prayed for his forgiveness and for God to allow him into heaven. That's when I forgave Daisy and the family member for the bad things that they did and allowed to happen to me.

Another special person in my life is Steve Harvey. I tell you, that guy has brought so much happiness into my life. When I was sad or depressed, I just went to YouTube to listen to his inspirational speeches and to look at his comedy shows. That's all it took because for some reason, he has that effect on most people, not just me.

The next special person in my life is Tyler Perry. Tyler Perry has been the most important guy in my life because when he speaks, he brings tears to my eyes, especially when he expresses to women about knowing our worth and loving ourselves. He also brought me closer to Daisy because of some of the words that he spoke and some of the videos and movies he has produced. Also, he made me reflect a lot and change some things in my life. He also taught me how to show my kids tough love, especially my son Righteous.

The last special person in my life is Oprah Winfrey. She's one of the strongest women I grew up knowing. I say that because she produced one of my favorite movies, which is a classic, *The Color Purple*. Oh my God! When I first saw that movie, I cried. But as I watched it, I became stronger. That movie taught me so much. It almost reminds me of my childhood. At the end of the movie, I learned that beauty lives inside of you and not on the outside. It doesn't matter how beautiful you are on the outside. These are some special people that God put in my path, whether watching them on television or hearing them on the radio.

Chapter 18

Turning Back to Religion

I started going attending church, but it wasn't the church I grew up in. All those members did was judge you by what you wore, or how you wore your hair. Yes, let's not forget about your past and how you kept coming to church and going to the altar. This made me feel very uncomfortable, so I stopped going to that church. I started having church at home, but they say church is within you. My entire life, I always felt like people judged me. But little did they know, I started to not care and turn bitter towards people. That only lasted for a little while because God didn't create me to be that way. I had a heart made of gold, and I always gave the clothes off my back. I know I'm not the only one who had a terrible childhood, but I have always been odd and different from everyone else. 1 Peter 2:9 NLT reads, "But you are not like that, for you are a chosen people. You are royal priests, a holy nation, God's very own possession."

One thing I can say is that God is good all the time, and I'm a living witness. God has brought me through so many trials and tribulations. I have passed some, and some I definitely failed. But I didn't keep disappointing God like others because I prayed and asked God to show me and guide me in the right direction. I remained to myself, for a while, until life took me on another journey.

Chapter 19

Learning How to Live in Peace

Having peace inside is the only way to enjoy life, and with that you have to believe in Christ. I always had faith because it comes from believing in your heart. Just like in the Bible, entering in God's rest is a faith that demands that we rest from relying on our own works. Living in peace, to me, is trying to stay in the Word, praying daily, staying away from drama and staying out of other people's business. Just be happy, live life to the fullest, and enjoy your family and friends. Teach other people about what you have learned and about how you became closer to God, after being a sinner all your life. Also, live for yourself and don't worry about what people say or care about you. No one can judge you; only God can judge. No one is perfect in this ungodly world. I guarantee you, not everyone who's in the church is living and walking a straight line as a Christian.

Acknowledgments

First and foremost, I want to thank God, who is the head of my life, for inspiring me to write this book. Next, I want to thank my children, who I love with all my heart, for bearing with me through some of my struggles, trials and tribulations, even though my life is not perfect. Throughout my life, I always kept you all first, and that's why I think God put this book in my soul and spirit to write about my life.

All I want my four children to know is, I did everything in my power to prevent them from any type of abusive situations occurring in their lives. I want to thank my companion for being loving and understanding while events unfolded as I wrote this book. I would also like to thank my dear friend for standing by me throughout the process of writing this book. I shared a lot of hidden pain with all of the people I named.

Lastly, I would like to acknowledge my mother, family,

friends and my associates for understanding and respecting my wishes about writing my book about my life. I also want to let anyone who is and was a part of my life know that I forgive them if they ever did anything to hurt or abuse our relationship. Also, I ask them to forgive me, as well, because that wasn't the real me; that was a person who was lost, confused and living life in the midst of pain, lies and betrayal.

About the Author

Tenika Timpson is a thirty-nine-year-old mother of four. Although she has endured many trials in her life, she doesn't wear them. She is grateful to God for this, and she shares her struggles with others so they will not fear coming out of their shells. God inspired her to write this book to be a blessing to those who share similar circumstances.

Ms. Timpson can be contacted at Tenikat33@icloud.com.

HadassahsCrownPublishing.com

Made in the USA
Middletown, DE
15 September 2022

10541148R00049